6 of The Best

Jamie Cullum

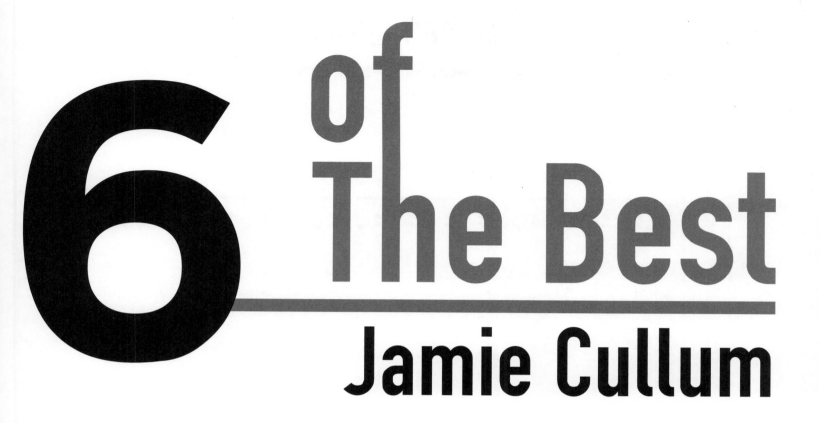

6 of The Best
Jamie Cullum

© 2010 by Faber Music Ltd
First published by Faber Music Ltd in 2010
Bloomsbury House 74–77 Great Russell Street London WC1B 3DA

Edited by Lucy Holliday & Alex Davis
New Arrangements by Olly Weeks
Designed by Lydia Merrills-Ashcroft
Photo © Douglas Mason/Getty Images

Printed in England by Caligraving Ltd
All rights reserved

The text paper used in this publication is a virgin fibre product
that is manufactured in the UK to ISO 14001 standards.
The wood fibre used is only sourced from managed forests using
sustainable forestry principles. This paper is 100% recyclable

ISBN10: 0-571-53587-9
EAN13: 978-0-571-53587-3

Reproducing this music in any form is illegal and forbidden by
the Copyright, Designs and Patents Act, 1988

To buy Faber Music publications or to find out about the full range
of titles available, please contact your local music retailer or
Faber Music sales enquiries:

Faber Music Ltd,
Burnt Mill, Elizabeth Way, Harlow, CM20 2HX England
Tel: +44(0)1279 82 89 82 Fax: +44(0)1279 82 89 83
sales@fabermusic.com fabermusic.com

CATCH THE SUN

Words and Music by Jimi Goodwin, Jez Williams and Andy Williams

1. Ev - 'ry day__ it comes__ to this, catch the things you might__ have missed you say__

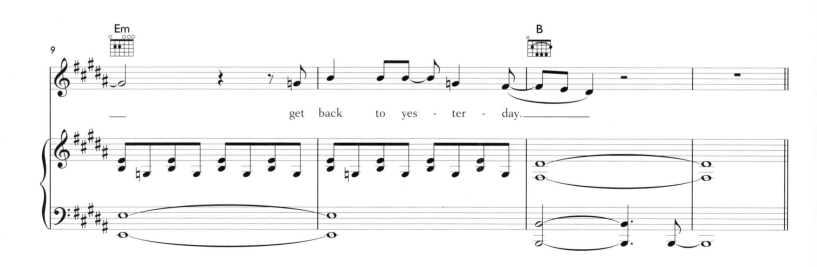

__ get back to yes - ter - day.__

DON'T STOP THE MUSIC

Words and Music by Michael Jackson, Mikkel Eriksen,
Tor Erik Hermansen and Frankie Storm

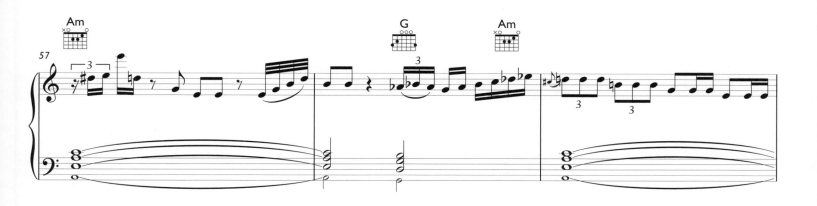

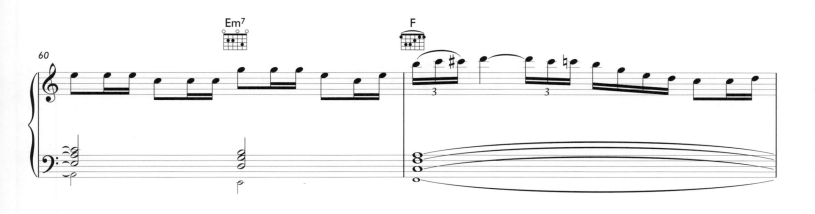

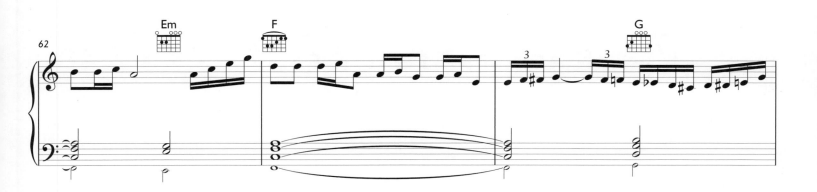

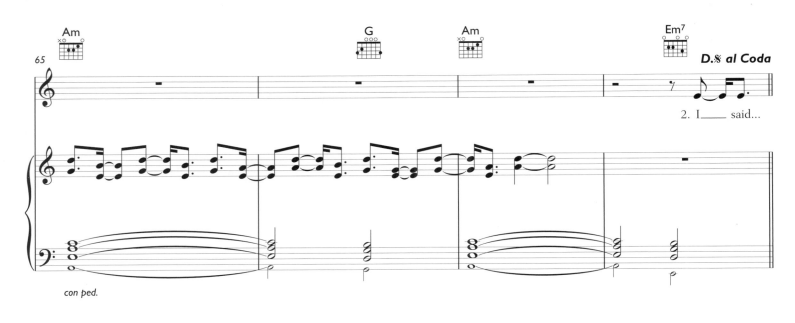

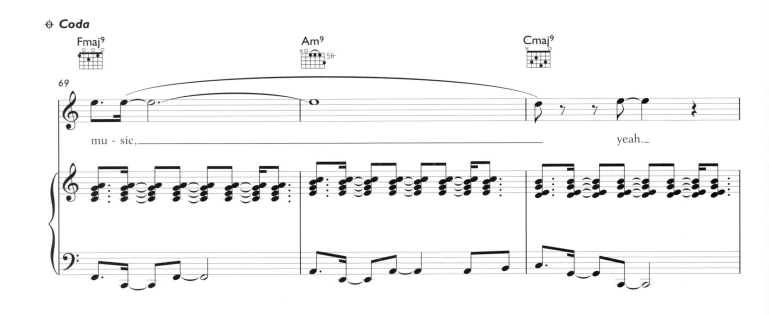

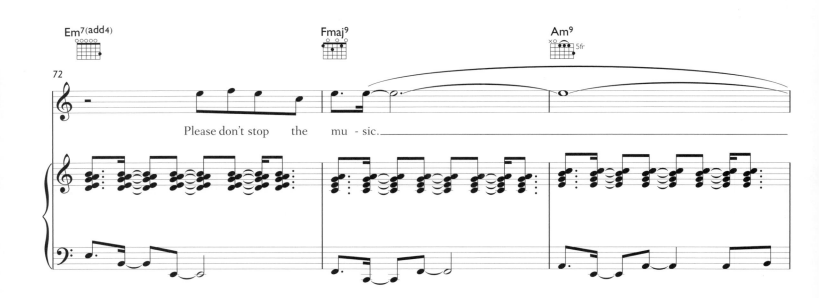

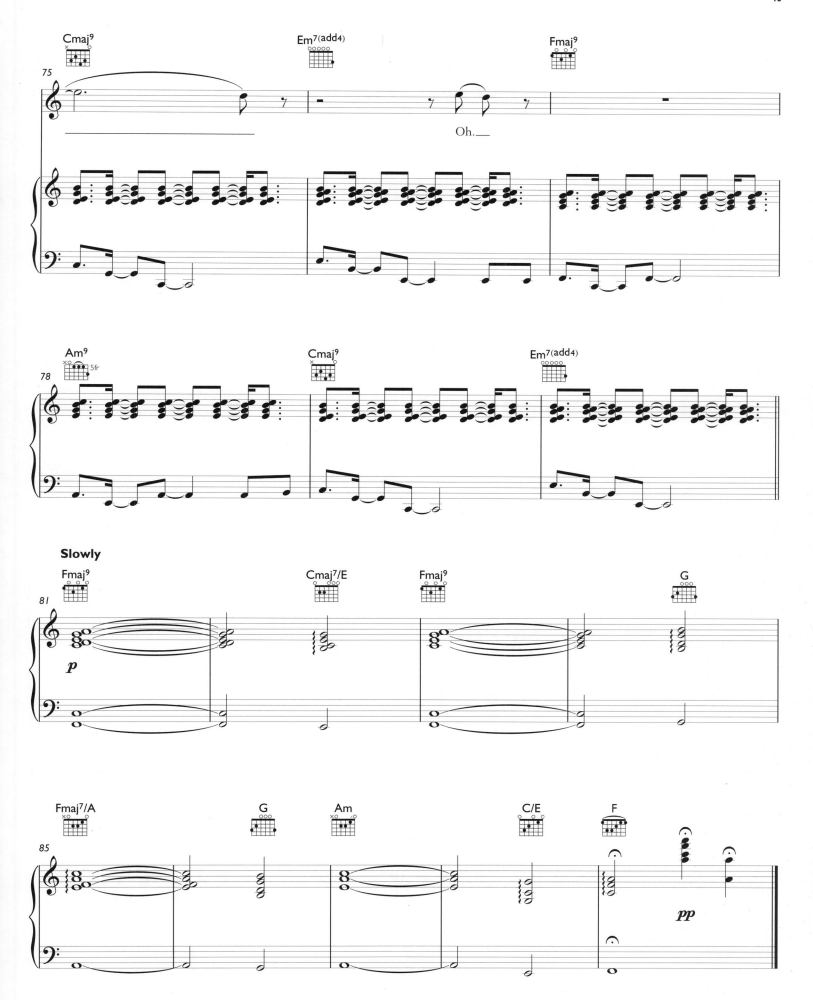

HIGH & DRY

Words and Music by Thomas Yorke, Jonathan Greenwood, Colin Greenwood, Edward O'Brien and Philip Selway

don't leave me dry,_____

don't leave me high,____

don't leave me__ dry.

I'M ALL OVER IT

Words and Music by Jamie Cullum and Ricky Ross

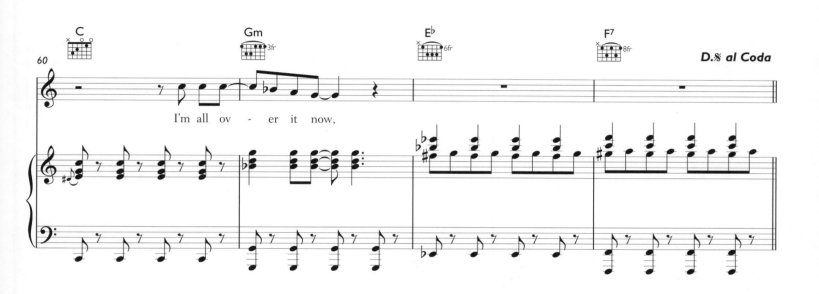

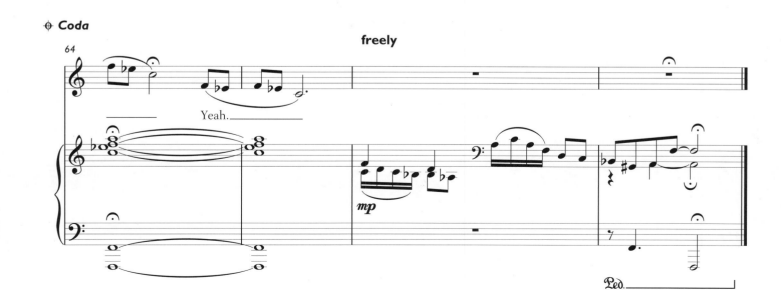

WHAT A DIFFERENCE A DAY MADE

Words by Stanley Adams
Music by Maria Grever

TWENTYSOMETHING

Words and Music by Jamie Cullum

I don't

want to get up___ just let me lie in;___ leave me a-lone___ I'm a twen-ty some-thing.___

Unaccompanied vocals

Do   do and do   do   and do and do do do do____ do and do   do   and do and do do do do...

Do   do and do   do   and do and do do do do____ do and do   do   and do and do do do do...

Do   do and do   do   and do and do do do do____ do and do   do   and do and do do do do_

____   do and do   do   and do and do do do do____ do and do   do   and do and do do do do.